If you've grown close to your inner child and found tokens of peace and emotional clarity through this shadow work journal, consider sharing your experience with us and others who may benefit from it. Your support means the world to us!

leave a review ♥

♪ 🅘 @zenfulnote

This journal is your new shadow work sidekick. It's full of introspective writing prompts, trigger tracking pages, and affirmations that will help you identify your shadows and build your emotional awareness.

WELCOME TO YOUR SHADOW SIDE

Hello reader. You have been divinely guided here, to this journal, and to this present moment.

You are seeking to KNOW yourself and you have made a conscious effort to begin *unraveling* the dualistic human experience that is called "life".

Life has brought you joy, sadness, confusion, pain, peace, wonder, happiness, and so on.

Your response to life is the greatest power you hold.

If you take the time to acknowledge how you respond, and when your shadows dictate your responses, you will begin to heal your inner child. Show your triggers compassion, attention, and care, and watch as they become less controlling over time.

Our hope is that the prompts and reflections in this journal shed light within your heart and assist in your inner-child healing.

Let's begin.

SET YOUR INTENTION

I, _____
set the intention to surrender completely to my
shadows and open my mind to exploring the depths of
who I am. I will come face-to-face with my ego and
surface the elements of my unconscious personality. I
vow to love and accept every part of my being, the
good and the bad. I know it may be a difficult time,
and I will show myself compassion in times of
frustration and pain. Today I reclaim my inner-child
and begin my shadow work journey.

WHAT IS SHADOW WORK?

Shadow Work was invented by Carl Jung, a Swiss psychiatrist, and psychoanalyst who founded analytical psychology. Carl Jung is recognized as one of the most influential psychiatrists of all time.
He founded analytical psychology and was one of the first experts in his field to explore the religious nature behind human psychology.

Simply put, your shadows are the least desirable parts of yourself that have been repressed over the course of your childhood.
Doing shadow work involves reflecting on memories and subjects that you least want to think about. It is not a "fun" practice, but if you are ready, shadow work is extremely rewarding, healing, and worth the effort.

Throughout life, you are consistently generating emotions based on your experiences. In some cases, you can process your feelings and learn from them.

In other cases, you fail to resolve and identify these emotions. When emotions from difficult situations are left unresolved, they hide away in the back of your subconscious as a shadow. Then, later in your life when a similar situation occurs, the shadows and negative reactions come along with it. To break this cycle, you must do what is called shadow work.

Examples of emotions that stem from your shadows are jealousy, sadness, rage, anger, pain, insecurity, stupidity, loneliness, vengeance, anxiousness, and fear. Shadow work does not feel good. Love, laughter, and confidence feel good. But to allow more good into your life, you must learn to know your full self and create the intention and space to heal the wounds that cast negativity onto your subconscious.

A GUIDE TO THIS JOURNAL:

This shadow work journal is broken up into 3 parts: inner child affirmations, journaling prompts, and trigger tracking pages.

INNER CHILD AFFIRMATIONS
Before diving into the other sections, warm your heart up to let your inner child in with some affirmations. There are 100 affirmations to choose from, so browse through the pages and affirm the phrases that speak to you.

TRIGGER TRACKING PAGES
The trigger tracking pages in this journal will be extremely beneficial to you in times of overwhelming emotional triggers. Remind yourself to fill out a tracking page to clear your head and face your shadows directly as they arise.

JOURNALING PROMPTS
The last section in this journal is filled with shadow work writing prompts. Find a quiet and comfortable setting, flip through all of the prompts and find one that you are called to. Some prompts may bring back painful memories and repressed emotions. Be sure to show yourself compassion, and practice self-care afterward.

PART 1
INNER-CHILD AFFIRMATIONS

INNER CHILD
AFFIRMATIONS

I am safe and protected

I show love to my inner child

I give myself space to heal

My childhood does not define me

I trust my inner child

I listen to my inner child's needs

I am worthy of love & support

I live with wonder and curiosity

I am where i'm supposed to be

Tomorrow is a new day

I am loved and accepted

I am in control of my reactions

I attract laughter and happiness

My thoughts are creating my future

My thoughts can be changed

I am divinely guided and protected

I nourish my body and mind

I see my own unique beauty

I forgive myself

I forgive others

I am in control of my thoughts

I let go of my doubts and worries

I am calm and collected

I have control over my mind

Everything is working out now

I am in flow with life

Good things are ahead

I choose happiness today

My body is relaxed

I trust myself and my intuition

I was made this way for a reason

I have a purpose

I make my child-self proud

I am kind and gentle to myself

I see beauty in life all around me

I decide what is important to me

Shame does not hold power over me

I am at peace

I am abundant

I am worthy of all good

What happened to me is real

I have the right to be heard

I can grieve as long as it takes

I show compassion to myself

I open my heart to feel peace

I am fully present in my body

I am emotionally safe

I am worthy to be cherished

I am connected to my inner self

I believe in ME

I let go of self-doubt

_____

I learn and grow everyday

_____

I am open to experiencing joy

_____

I find beauty in the small things

_____

I am curious and compassionate

_____

I practice self-love

_____

I have the tools I need to heal

_____

I can ask for help

_____

I am equipped to face challenges

_____

There is more good inside of me

_____

I manage my feelings

_____

Things will work out

_____

I can face any challenge

_____

I thrive as myself

_____

My anxiety does not define me

_____

I take it one day at a time

_____

I attract love and laughter

_____

I have the courage to say no

_____

I am a positive person

_____

I accept myself as I am

_____

I am surrounded by light

_____

I am in control of my actions

_____

I am in control of my thoughts

_____

I am healing and learning

_____

I accept who I am

_____

I am in touch with my emotions

_____

I listen to my child-self

_____

I give myself love and care

_____

I am not afraid to seek help

_____

I am whole and complete

_____

I forgive myself

I am healing and growing

I am loved

I am fearless and brave

My thoughts are changing for the better

I set myself free

I am divinely guided

I am present here and now

I am content with what I have

I am a valuable human being

I am more than enough

_____

I am calm and mindful

_____

I look fondly upon memories of my past

_____

I'm doing the best I can

_____

I am proud of myself

_____

I love who I am becoming

_____

I am filled with healing light

_____

I am at peace with my failures and mistakes

_____

My heart is pure

_____

I am so grateful for my life

_____

I know my worth

I am so proud of my growth

Success comes to me easily

I find peace all around me

I am grateful for my personality

I am worthy of all my desires

I am healing, I am safe

I am not alone in my struggles

I am in control

I love my child-self

PART 2
SHADOW WORK PROMPTS

MEET YOUR INNER-CHILD

What activities did you enjoy as a child? What stories did you enjoy listening to? What does this reveal about your inner-child?

5 LIVES TO LIVE

If you had 5 imaginary lives to live, what would you do and be like in each one of them?

SPEAK TO YOUR CHILD-SELF

If you could speak to your child-self,
what would you tell them?

A LETTER TO YOUR PAST-SELF

If you could speak to your past-self, what would you say? Write a letter to them.

A FOND MEMORY IN YOUR CHILDHOOD

Think back to a time as a child when you felt
the most joyous. Write about this memory below.

A PAINFUL
CHILDHOOD MEMORY

Think back to a time you felt hurt as a child.
Imagine you could speak to your child-self at that
moment- what would you tell them?

YOUR CHILDHOOD FEARS

Reflect on your childhood fears, both physical and emotional. Where do these fears stem from?

WHO WAS YOUR CHILD-SELF?

What were you like as a child?
Describe your traits, interests, and emotions.
What were your favorite toys and activities?

MEMORIES THAT BRING GUILT

Write about a time when you felt guilt.
What was happening? What do you wish you did
differently?

FEELING SAFE +
AT PEACE

Write about a time you felt a strong sense of safety
and protection that brought you peace.

FEELING BELOW OTHERS

In what areas of life do you feel below
or inferior to others?

ENVY + JEALOUSY

Is there a certain person you envy?
When do you catch yourself being jealous? Why?

YOUR DREAM LIFE

Imagine that tomorrow you will wake up and live
your dream life. What does your day look like?

TRAITS FROM YOUR PARENTS

Write about the traits and mannerisms that you have inherited from your parents or guardians.

WHAT YOU ARE PASSIONATE ABOUT?

What hobbies, subjects, or areas of life bring you the greatest sense of purpose?

DRAINING YOUR ENERGY

What drains your energy?
Why does this drain your energy?
How do you cope?

THINGS THAT BRING YOU ENERGY

When do you feel the most energized?

JUDGMENT FOR OTHERS
AND YOURSELF

Write about instances where you have judged
others. Have you done the same?

CHILDHOOD NEEDS

What did you lack in your childhood?
How do you think this influences you today?

YOUR SELF-PERSONA

How do you view yourself?
How do you think the world views you?
What do you wish more people knew about you?

YOUR INNER VOICE

What does the voice in your head sound like?
Is your inner voice kind or mean? Why?

UNCOMFORTABLE SITUATIONS

What situations or environments make you uncomfortable? Why? How do you cope?

ANXIETY AND OVERTHINKING

Write about a few scenarios where you have experienced anxiety. Why were you anxious?

I WISH I WAS MORE...

What traits do you see in others that you wish
you had more of? How can you be gracious and
accept yourself as you are?

SETTING STRONG BOUNDARIES

Do you set boundaries for yourself?
If not, where do you see the need to?

THE COLOR OF ANXIETY

What color represents your anxiety? Why?

PERSONAL CHANGE

What are 5 ways you have changed in the last 5 years?

YOUR INSECURITIES

WHAT ARE YOUR BIGGEST INSECURITIES?

How can you show these parts of yourself more love?

FEELING FREEDOM

WHEN DO YOU FEEL THE MOST FREEDOM?

Think about feeling completely free.
What images or memories come to mind?

CAUSING PAIN TO OTHERS

HAVE YOU CAUSED OTHER PEOPLE PAIN?

How can you be more compassionate towards others?

A LETTER TO YOUR FUTURE SELF

Imagine if you could speak to the future you.
Write a letter to them.

YOUR PERSONAL VALUES

What are your core values?
Why are these so important to you?

SHOWING YOURSELF LOVE

HOW DO YOU PRACTICE SELF-LOVE?

What do you do to show yourself love?
How often do you practice self-care?

CONFRONTING OTHERS

When do you feel the need to confront others?
Are you comfortable with confrontation or not?

FACING YOUR LAST BREATH

IMAGINE YOU WERE ON YOUR DEATHBED TODAY.
While laying in bed, your parents walk in. What are the last things you say to them?

EXPERIENCING LONELINESS

When do you feel lonely?
Does being alone make you uncomfortable?
Do you feel alone around others?

SOCIALIZING WITH OTHERS

How often do you socialize with others?
Do you experience anxiety or energy around people?

A TIME OF DISAPPOINTMENT

Write about a time when someone you looked up to disappointed you.

A LETTER TO YOUR ANCESTORS

Do you have questions for them?
What do you want them to know?

THE COLOR OF SADNESS

What color represents your sadness? Why?

YOUR PARENTS'
VALUES

What were your parents'/guardians core
values growing up as a child?
How has this influenced you?

EXPERIENCING JOY

When was the last time you experienced joy?
Why did you feel joyful?

A LETTER TO SOMEONE YOU LOVE

Write a letter to someone who you love dearly.

EXPERIENCING
ANGER

How do you express anger? Do you bottle your
anger up or blame others for causing it?

BEING HARD ON YOURSELF

When are you hardest on yourself? Why do you feel
the need to put this pressure on yourself?

A BOOK ABOUT YOUR LIFE

If you were to write a book about your life,
what would the title be? Why?

LOSING TRACK OF TIME

What could you do all day long without feeling the time pass?

QUOTES

What are your favorite quotes?
Why do these resonate so much with you?

PEOPLE WHO'VE IMPACTED YOU

Which people have left the biggest impact on your life? Have they left a positive or negative impact?

STRESS

WHAT BRINGS YOU STRESS?

Think back to a time when your stress about
a certain situation kept you up at night.
What happened? What was the outcome?

A LETTER TO SOMEONE WHO HURT YOU

Write a letter to someone who hurt you.

YOUR DAYDREAM

What do you love to do or daydream about no matter how silly/irrelevant it feels to you now?

CENSORING YOURSELF

What causes you to conceal or censor yourself?

EXPERIENCING
SADNESS

When was the last time you experienced sadness?

FEELING SAFE

What makes you feel safe and protected?

THE COLOR OF HEALING

What color represents your healing?
Why that color?

FEELING UNSAFE

What makes you feel unsafe and vulnerable?

YOUR INNER-CHILD NEEDS

In what way is your inner child effecting
your life right now?

THE COLOR OF PAIN

What color represents your pain? Why?

PART 3
TRACK YOUR TRIGGERS

TRACK YOUR TRIGGERS

Event
What happened?

Feelings
How did it make me feel?

Thoughts
What are my thoughts?

Healing
What can I do to feel better?

dig inside this heart -
find me where I am most bruised

love me there.

TRACK YOUR TRIGGERS

Event
What happened?

Feelings
How did it make me feel?

Thoughts
What are my thoughts?

Healing
What can I do to feel better?

TRACK YOUR TRIGGERS

Event
What happened?

Feelings
How did it make me feel?

Thoughts
What are my thoughts?

Healing
What can I do to feel better?

TRACK YOUR TRIGGERS

Event
What happened?

Feelings
How did it make me feel?

Thoughts
What are my thoughts?

Healing
What can I do to feel better?

place healing words
in your heart's open wounds
and one day

you will feel your
wholeness again.

TRACK YOUR TRIGGERS

Event
What happened?

Feelings
How did it make me feel?

Thoughts
What are my thoughts?

Healing
What can I do to feel better?

TRACK YOUR TRIGGERS

Event
What happened?

Feelings
How did it make me feel?

Thoughts
What are my thoughts?

Healing
What can I do to feel better?

TRACK YOUR TRIGGERS

Event
What happened?

Feelings
How did it make me feel?

Thoughts
What are my thoughts?

Healing
What can I do to feel better?

be easy.
take your time.
you are on your way home
to yourself.

TRACK YOUR TRIGGERS

Event
What happened?

Feelings
How did it make me feel?

Thoughts
What are my thoughts?

Healing
What can I do to feel better?

TRACK YOUR TRIGGERS

Event
What happened?

Feelings
How did it make me feel?

Thoughts
What are my thoughts?

Healing
What can I do to feel better?

TRACK YOUR TRIGGERS

Event
What happened?

Feelings
How did it make me feel?

Thoughts
What are my thoughts?

Healing
What can I do to feel better?

TRACK YOUR TRIGGERS

Event
What happened?

Feelings
How did it make me feel?

Thoughts
What are my thoughts?

Healing
What can I do to feel better?

TRACK YOUR TRIGGERS

Event
What happened?

Feelings
How did it make me feel?

Thoughts
What are my thoughts?

Healing
What can I do to feel better?

you are
more than your failure
more than your pain
you are *love*

TRACK YOUR TRIGGERS

Event
What happened?

Feelings
How did it make me feel?

Thoughts
What are my thoughts?

Healing
What can I do to feel better?

TRACK YOUR TRIGGERS

Event
What happened?

Feelings
How did it make me feel?

Thoughts
What are my thoughts?

Healing
What can I do to feel better?

TRACK YOUR TRIGGERS

Event
What happened?

Feelings
How did it make me feel?

Thoughts
What are my thoughts?

Healing
What can I do to feel better?

TRACK YOUR TRIGGERS

Event
What happened?

Feelings
How did it make me feel?

Thoughts
What are my thoughts?

Healing
What can I do to feel better?

TRACK YOUR TRIGGERS

Event
What happened?

Feelings
How did it make me feel?

Thoughts
What are my thoughts?

Healing
What can I do to feel better?

TRACK YOUR TRIGGERS

Event
What happened?

Feelings
How did it make me feel?

Thoughts
What are my thoughts?

Healing
What can I do to feel better?

you'll find your greatest enemy
in your darkest shadows
and in befriending them
you will be at peace with
every part of you.

TRACK YOUR TRIGGERS

Event
What happened?

Feelings
How did it make me feel?

Thoughts
What are my thoughts?

Healing
What can I do to feel better?

TRACK YOUR TRIGGERS

Event
What happened?

Feelings
How did it make me feel?

Thoughts
What are my thoughts?

Healing
What can I do to feel better?

TRACK YOUR TRIGGERS

Event
What happened?

Feelings
How did it make me feel?

Thoughts
What are my thoughts?

Healing
What can I do to feel better?

TRACK YOUR TRIGGERS

Event
What happened?

Feelings
How did it make me feel?

Thoughts
What are my thoughts?

Healing
What can I do to feel better?

TRACK YOUR TRIGGERS

Event
What happened?

Feelings
How did it make me feel?

Thoughts
What are my thoughts?

Healing
What can I do to feel better?

TRACK YOUR TRIGGERS

Event
What happened?

Feelings
How did it make me feel?

Thoughts
What are my thoughts?

Healing
What can I do to feel better?

TRACK YOUR TRIGGERS

Event
What happened?

Feelings
How did it make me feel?

Thoughts
What are my thoughts?

Healing
What can I do to feel better?

TRACK YOUR TRIGGERS

Event
What happened?

Feelings
How did it make me feel?

Thoughts
What are my thoughts?

Healing
What can I do to feel better?

smile at the fear
smile at the pain
just as a mother would
to her baby's cry
you will tend to every wound
and listen to the child inside.

TRACK YOUR TRIGGERS

Event
What happened?

Feelings
How did it make me feel?

Thoughts
What are my thoughts?

Healing
What can I do to feel better?

TRACK YOUR TRIGGERS

Event
What happened?

Feelings
How did it make me feel?

Thoughts
What are my thoughts?

Healing
What can I do to feel better?

TRACK YOUR TRIGGERS

Event
What happened?

Feelings
How did it make me feel?

Thoughts
What are my thoughts?

Healing
What can I do to feel better?

TRACK YOUR TRIGGERS

Event

What happened?

Feelings

How did it make me feel?

Thoughts

What are my thoughts?

Healing

What can I do to feel better?

TRACK YOUR TRIGGERS

Event
What happened?

Feelings
How did it make me feel?

Thoughts
What are my thoughts?

Healing
What can I do to feel better?

arms and chest wide open;
like a vial without
a lid
surrender to the light
and you'll find that the emptiness
is part of what makes you whole

TRACK YOUR TRIGGERS

Event
What happened?

Feelings
How did it make me feel?

Thoughts
What are my thoughts?

Healing
What can I do to feel better?

TRACK YOUR TRIGGERS

Event
What happened?

Feelings
How did it make me feel?

Thoughts
What are my thoughts?

Healing
What can I do to feel better?

TRACK YOUR TRIGGERS

Event
What happened?

Feelings
How did it make me feel?

Thoughts
What are my thoughts?

Healing
What can I do to feel better?

the process of healing
is not complete when the wounds are covered
and no longer visible to the eye.
healing is when
you frame your wounds on the wall
and admire them with compassion
they made you
strong

TRACK YOUR TRIGGERS

Event
What happened?

Feelings
How did it make me feel?

Thoughts
What are my thoughts?

Healing
What can I do to feel better?

TRACK YOUR TRIGGERS

Event
What happened?

Feelings
How did it make me feel?

Thoughts
What are my thoughts?

Healing
What can I do to feel better?

TRACK YOUR TRIGGERS

Event
What happened?

Feelings
How did it make me feel?

Thoughts
What are my thoughts?

Healing
What can I do to feel better?

TRACK YOUR TRIGGERS

Event
What happened?

Feelings
How did it make me feel?

Thoughts
What are my thoughts?

Healing
What can I do to feel better?

TRACK YOUR TRIGGERS

Event
What happened?

Feelings
How did it make me feel?

Thoughts
What are my thoughts?

Healing
What can I do to feel better?

TRACK YOUR TRIGGERS

Event

What happened?

Feelings

How did it make me feel?

Thoughts

What are my thoughts?

Healing

What can I do to feel better?

TRACK YOUR TRIGGERS

Event
What happened?

Feelings
How did it make me feel?

Thoughts
What are my thoughts?

Healing
What can I do to feel better?

TRACK YOUR TRIGGERS

Event
What happened?

Feelings
How did it make me feel?

Thoughts
What are my thoughts?

Healing
What can I do to feel better?

healing is
a gentle
crushing
intimate
painful
story.

what will you name yours?

TRACK YOUR TRIGGERS

Event
What happened?

Feelings
How did it make me feel?

Thoughts
What are my thoughts?

Healing
What can I do to feel better?

TRACK YOUR TRIGGERS

Event
What happened?

Feelings
How did it make me feel?

Thoughts
What are my thoughts?

Healing
What can I do to feel better?

TRACK YOUR TRIGGERS

Event
What happened?

Feelings
How did it make me feel?

Thoughts
What are my thoughts?

Healing
What can I do to feel better?

TRACK YOUR TRIGGERS

Event
What happened?

Feelings
How did it make me feel?

Thoughts
What are my thoughts?

Healing
What can I do to feel better?

TRACK YOUR TRIGGERS

Event
What happened?

Feelings
How did it make me feel?

Thoughts
What are my thoughts?

Healing
What can I do to feel better?

TRACK YOUR TRIGGERS

Event
What happened?

Feelings
How did it make me feel?

Thoughts
What are my thoughts?

Healing
What can I do to feel better?

your inner-child is glowing
deep inside your heart
telling you the secrets
that made her from the start
she giggles at the heartbeats
strong, fast, alert
her gentle presence soothes you
and calms down your nerves.

remember her

TRACK YOUR TRIGGERS

Event
What happened?

Feelings
How did it make me feel?

Thoughts
What are my thoughts?

Healing
What can I do to feel better?

TRACK YOUR TRIGGERS

Event

What happened?

Feelings

How did it make me feel?

Thoughts

What are my thoughts?

Healing

What can I do to feel better?

TRACK YOUR TRIGGERS

Event
What happened?

Feelings
How did it make me feel?

Thoughts
What are my thoughts?

Healing
What can I do to feel better?

TRACK YOUR TRIGGERS

Event
What happened?

Feelings
How did it make me feel?

Thoughts
What are my thoughts?

Healing
What can I do to feel better?

they broke you so that
you could find yourself again
but this time you are healed.

magic puzzles

If you've grown close to your inner child and found tokens of peace and emotional clarity through this shadow work journal, consider sharing your experience with us and others who may benefit from it. Your support means the world to us!

leave a review 🖤

Made in United States
Troutdale, OR
08/28/2023

12415741R00086